BYZANTIUM

ART OF THE WORLD

A SERIES OF REGIONAL HISTORIES
OF THE VISUAL ARTS

BYZANTIUM

BYZANTINE ART IN THE MIDDLE AGES

ANDRÉ GRABAR

METHUEN–LONDON

FIRST PUBLISHED IN 1963

© HOLLE VERLAG G.M.B.H., BADEN-BADEN, GERMANY

FIRST PUBLISHED IN GREAT BRITAIN IN 1966

ENGLISH TRANSLATION © 1966 BY METHUEN & CO. LTD.

PRINTED IN HOLLAND

Translated by Betty Forster

Title-page: *Christ Pantocrator.*
Mosaic in the dome of the cathedral at Arta in Epirus, ca. 1300.

CONTENTS

LIST OF PLATES

LIST OF PLANS

MAP

8

ACKNOWLEDGEMENTS

The following libraries and museums kindly allowed reproduction of the works represented in the plates on the following pages:

Bibliothèque Nationale, Paris 23, 31, 34, 39, 61, 71, 143, 147, 153, 161, 163

Byzantine Museum, Athens 195

Cabinet des Médailles, Paris 43, 167

Laurentian Library, Florence 55, 156

Marcian Library, Venice 57, 175

Museo Sacro, Vatican 191

National Library, Vienna 21

Palatine Library, Parma 159

Treasury of St. Mark's, Venice 19, 41, 59, 171

Vatican Library 53, 145, 151

The plates on the following pages were taken and kindly made available by:

Mme. Florand 3, 27, 29, 49, 51, 64, 75, 83, 95, 125, 133, 135, 137, 139

Mme. Hassia 193, 195

J. Powell 97, 131, 183, 185, 187, 189

M. and Mme. Thierry 25, 67, 141

The other plates, taken by Mlle. D. Fourmont, belong to the Ecole des Hautes Etudes, Paris.

The plans were kindly drawn by M. A. Khatchatrian.

TRANSLATOR'S NOTE

In the spelling of names Latinized forms have generally been preferred to those from the Greek.

THE BYZANTINE EMPIRE IN THE MIDDLE AGES

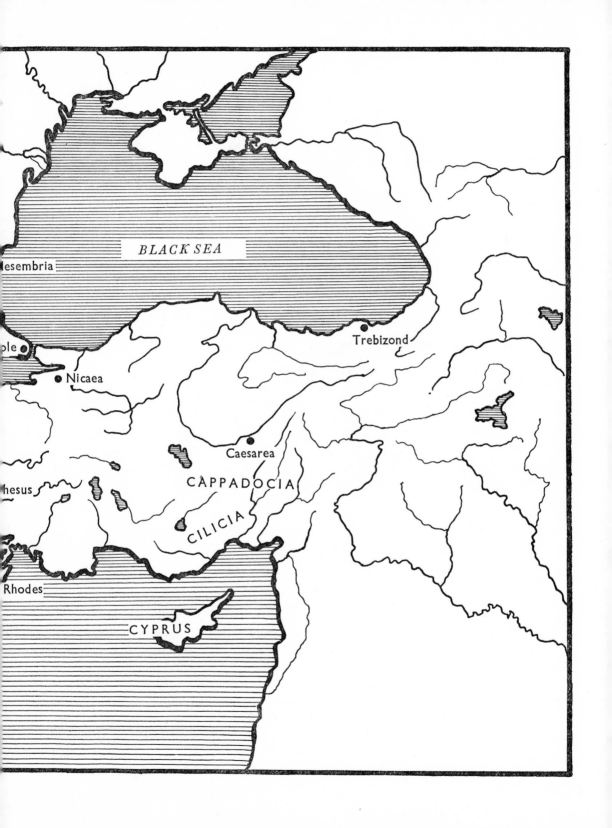

Mesembria

BLACK SEA

ple

Nicaea

Trebizond

Caesarea

hesus

CAPPADOCIA

CILICIA

Rhodes

CYPRUS

PART I

GENERAL CHARACTERISTICS OF BYZANTINE ART

I. THE GEOGRAPHICAL
AND HISTORICAL FRAMEWORK

The aim of this book is to present and study Byzantine medieval art, the origins of which go back to the Iconoclasts (762–843), and which in principle stops with the fall of the East Christian Empire and the capture of Constantinople by the Turks in 1543.

It is evident that these limits are somewhat theoretical. There were, before the year 726, works of Byzantine art which heralded the Middle Ages — and the disappearance of the Byzantine state in 1453 did not mean that at that date all artistic activity faithful to the Byzantine tradition ceased. We shall often be writing of the Byzantine traditions established before the Iconoclast period which maintained and renewed themselves during the period we are to study. It seems useful to state from the beginning that the history of Byzantine art during the period which stretches from the end of antiquity to the eve of modern times presents a far greater continuity than the history of Western art during the same period. We will explain later the reasons for this continuity. Nevertheless in Byzantium, as in the West, art as practised during the Middle Ages had its own characteristics, which it is useful and fair to separate from those of the art which was practised previously — between the reign of Constantine, who founded Constantinople in 330, and the beginnings of the Iconoclast crisis (330–726). It is entirely to medieval art that we are going to devote ourselves, returning to its origins only where it may help us to a better understanding of medieval Byzantine works and the artistic life of Constantinople during the Middle Ages.

Individuality of medieval Byzantine art

When one tries to imagine the territory over which the artistic works of the Byzantines stretched during the period we are studying, one naturally thinks of Constantinople, of Greece with its islands, and of the whole of the Mediterranean provinces around the capital on the Bosphorus. This summary description of the area in which Byzantine artists were active is not false, but it requires more precise definition. One must above all remember the essential fact that

Geographical spread of Byzantine art

Byzantine territory itself and that of the area it influenced in matters of art and culture did not remain the same between 726 and 1453. From the end of antiquity to the period of the foundation of Constantinople, and again in the sixth century under Justinian and his successors, the art which was to remain the basis of Byzantine art was practised, with fairly evident regional differences, in the whole eastern half of the Roman Empire, which then stretched as *Successive reductions of* far as the Euphrates and upper Mesopotamia, and as far as the *Byzantine Empire* Nubian desert in Egypt. The Arab conquest in the seventh century removed Egypt, Syria and a part of Asia Minor so that the Byzantine Empire was reduced by half and came to be concentrated around the Greek lands. It then became definitely hellenized and kept to the very end that ethnic and cultural predominance of things Greek, to the detriment of the Latin element which the Roman conquests had established everywhere around the Mediterranean. It also discarded the Semitic elements which, after the annexation of the countries of the Levant by Rome, had played an active part in the development of the empire.

While the Arabs seized from Byzantium her rich provinces in the Levant, the Lombards reduced her Italian possessions and the Bulgars crossed the Danube and settled in the north-eastern Balkans, where Slav infiltration spread progressively, reaching the shores of Salonika (Thessalonica) and the core of the oldest Greek provinces. At times Arabs, Khazars, and Bulgarians ventured as far as the gates of Constantinople and endangered the very existence of the Byzantine state. The historical role of the emperors of the eighth and *The 'Iconoclast'* the beginning of the ninth centuries was to have stopped these in- *emperors* vasions, and to have ensured the survival of the Christian empire of Byzantium. The attack against images which they launched at the same time, undoubtedly with military reasons in mind (in order to ensure the active participation of the Christians of eastern Asia Minor — a frontier district, where the fate of the empire was at stake), earned them the title of Iconoclasts. This sobriquet, although a questionable one if we take into consideration the whole of their work, does however describe one particular aspect of their reign — their religious and artistic activities. We shall return to this point, only observing in passing their opposition as emperors to images —

an attitude taken up in defence of Byzantine territory at the period when it was most reduced.

Their military successes, which were continued and increased during the rule of the Amorian (820–867) and particularly the Macedonian dynasty (867–1056), gave back to Byzantium a political stability which she was losing, and at the same time remarkable economic strength and great international prestige. For several centuries the empire of Constantinople again became the most important power in the Mediterranean world; but its territory was not significantly increased as compared with the Iconoclast period. There were of course brilliant reconquests in the tenth century, some temporary, others permanent, in the direction of Armenia, Syria and even Palestine, under Nicephorus Phocas and John Tzimisces, and other reconquests at the beginning of the eleventh century towards Bulgaria, Dalmatia and even southern Italy. But these territorial extensions of the empire — which play a part in the history of art through Byzantine institutions in these territories being brought back to the mother country — were not to be maintained. A terrible defeat of the Byzantine armies by the Turks in 1071 and the development of the Slav kingdoms in the Balkans in the twelfth century prevented Byzantium from holding on to them. So one can say that, from the fall of the Iconoclasts (843) to the end of the twelfth century, the area of Byzantine expansion remained essentially the same. Roughly speaking, it included on one hand all the territory between Dalmatia and the lower Danube, and on the other the southern extremity of the Greek archipelago, as well as the western part of Asia Minor and its coastal regions, up to and including Trebizond in the north and Antioch in the south.

During the twelfth century the territorial problems of the Byzantine state became complicated by frequent campaigns against the Serbian and particularly Norman kings, and by the Crusaders crossing and sometimes fighting their way through the countries of the Byzantine empire. They even carved out for themselves fiefs in the Antioch area, whereas the Armenian princes, who had taken refuge from the Turks, made of the Byzantine province of Cilicia a 'little Armenia'. But for the study of art the passage to and fro of foreign armies, the political insecurity, and the more or less short-

Amorian and Macedonian dynasties

Territories of the Byzantine Empire from the Xth to the XIIth century

lived changes in sovereignty which they brought about in one or other of the frontier provinces, are of little importance. For in all these territories within the area just described, quite independently of the politico-geographical fluctuations, it was the same Byzantine art that was invariably practised, whether it was executed by the Byzantines themselves or by those who tried, and often succeeded, in displacing them politically from these provinces.

In other words, from the point of view of artistic geography, Byzantium enjoyed such a true predominance in culture and in technical skills, and such prestige in the artistic field, that the area of its artistic expansion spread constantly beyond the frontiers of the Byzantine state. The main agents of this expansion were the Greek Christians established in foreign countries — and the foreign Christians converted by Byzantine missions. This was the case in Syria, Armenia and southern Italy on one hand, and in Georgia and the Slav countries on the other. The mission to the Slavs was particularly fruitful from this point of view. If politically, during the period under review, the territory of the Byzantine Empire increased only occasionally and then for a short time, it did however undergo an extraordinary expansion between the end of the ninth and the end of the tenth centuries, following the religious conquest of all the Balkan countries, and of the whole of Russia. This time it was the field of religious (not political) conquest which served as a background to the widespread influence of art. If there is one sphere where the progress of Byzantium is a reality, and compensates for so many territorial withdrawals since the seventh century, it is in the

field of art. From the ninth century onwards the Orthodox religion, directed with a firm hand by the Church of Constantinople, was an important vehicle in the spreading of this art beyond the borders of the Byzantine state. It was to continue to play this role, even to an enhanced extent, during the periods when the political power of the Byzantine state suffered an eclipse.

We must here note this fact, which is an important one for appreciating the exceptional part played by Byzantine art in the Middle Ages. But in this book we shall only concern ourselves with truly Byzantine works, reserving the study of art in the different countries of Eastern Europe for another volume in this series.

PLATE I – Two military saints. Detail of an icon, XIth-century enamel. *Treasury of St. Mark's, Venice.*
Cf. p. 40

It is from the twelfth century onwards that one witnesses the divorce between the Byzantine state and the art which it had promoted, the immense territorial extent of the latter having no common measure with the very reduced territory of the empire under the Comneni and the Angeli (1081–1185, 1185–1204). Admittedly it was the Comneni who reconquered the easternmost part of the southern coast of Asia Minor, as far as and including Antioch. But this modest increase in imperial territory did not spread beyond the districts of neighbouring Cappadocia, where however the execution of art in the Byzantine tradition continued even though the country was part of the Turkish sultanate of Iconium.

The Comneni and the Angeli

Fourth Crusade

In 1204, diverted from its real aim, the Fourth Crusade took Constantinople and devastated it. While the Byzantine state, Greek and Orthodox, reconstituted itself on the Asiatic coast of the Bosphorus around the city of Nicaea, the conquerors of 1204 attempted to found a Latin and Catholic empire based on Constantinople. This state, organized on the Western pattern of the period, was bordered by a series of feudal principalities covering practically the whole territory of continental Greece and its islands; it did not resist long attempts at reconquest led by the exiled Greek emperors in Nicaea.

Reconquest of Constantinople by emperors of Nicaea

In 1261 the latter returned to Constantinople, reconstituting the link with the Byzantine past. We know practically nothing of Greek artistic activities during the Latin Empire. This is perhaps due in part to the accidental destruction of works of art which date from that half-century. One may of course ask oneself whether an art, which at that period was exclusively religious, must not have been dimmed by the brutal installation of the Latin clergy in Constantinople and the forced withdrawal of the Greek clergy and of those who, by the means at their disposal and their influence, were the traditional patrons of Byzantine artistic works — that is to say, the emperors and the aristocracy of Byzantium. The Latin domination, which in Constantinople and its district lasted for half a century and even longer in certain parts of Greece and in the islands, left remarkably few traces of monuments. This fact is very striking when one thinks of the considerable and simultaneous expansion of

PLATE 7 – Victory of Constantine on the Milvius Bridge before Rome. Miniature, ca. 885. *Bibliothèque Nationale, Paris (MS. Grec 510). Cf. p. 152*

individual temperament or passing sentiment are hardly reflected. This form of art in no way attempts to tell us about the man who initiated it in these regular conditions. If the artist should of necessity express himself, the margin of his intervention is rather narrow and generally limited to nuances of style. It would also be fruitless to look in these Byzantine works, by analysing the subject of the paintings or bas-reliefs, for references to men and to the world in which they lived. There are no such references, no details taken from life, no indiscretions which might indicate the social class or the geographical origin of their authors. Byzantine images, even those which served as illustrations for chronicles, always kept their distance from reality. It is easier to understand the reason for this when saints or sacred events are represented: the irrational is expressed by establishing a distance between the image and material reality. But secular or profane images are just as slow to reflect reality. They remain brief and vague, and impress one by the very absence of sharpness in the reproduction of beings and objects pertaining to everyday life: they are 'symbols' rather than representations. Here we touch upon an essential characteristic of Byzantine art — one which is in opposition both to Muslim and Western art.

This conception of artistic representation in relation to transitory life and the things which support that life, explains what we were saying earlier on: that Byzantine art is difficult to integrate into the historical and geographical background. It touches lightly on what is accidental, including the fate of the individual and even events which are of interest to society. It had its proper role and went its own way. This is a feature to which we will return later. Very exceptional circumstances (such as the Iconoclast edicts of the emperors of the eighth and ninth centuries) were necessary to change this even temporarily. Other happenings did not affect them, and it shows a certain lack of 'historical sense' to expect Byzantine works to provide direct evidence about the social and economic history of Byzantium in the Middle Ages, or about the reactions of a class or an individual to any given event of history, including even religious history.

The overwhelming majority of Byzantine works of art were created